Henry Albert Hinkson

Student Life in Trinity College, Dublin

Henry Albert Hinkson

Student Life in Trinity College, Dublin

ISBN/EAN: 9783743433069

Manufactured in Europe, USA, Canada, Australia, Japa

Cover: Foto ©ninafisch / pixelio.de

Manufactured and distributed by brebook publishing software (www.brebook.com)

Henry Albert Hinkson

Student Life in Trinity College, Dublin

Student Life

IN

TRINITY COLLEGE, DUBLIN.

BY

H. A. HINKSON.

With Illustrations

BY

WALTER C. MILLS

(Daily Graphic.)

DUBLIN: J. CHARLES & SON
61, MIDDLE ABBEY STREET

1892

J. CHARLES AND SON, PRINTERS, MIDDLE ABBEY STREET, DUBLIN.

PREFACE.

THE Contents of this little book are with some alterations and additions, reprinted from a series of articles, which appeared in the "*Evening Herald*" during the present year, and which, through the courtesy of Mr. Moore, the Editor, I am enabled to publish in this present form. The aim of the book is to give some notion of College life from a Student's point of view, and the author claims no special qualification for the task he has set himself, save that having lived more than five years within the walls of Trinity College he has had ample opportunity both in his own person and as an observer of others, of noting both the joys and the sorrows of a Student's life.

Bearing in mind, too, the familiar estimate made by Carlyle, of the intellectual capacity of the British Isles, and being desirous of catering for the tastes of the majority, he has in an access of philanthropy determined to provide, by the insertion of advertisements, a mental pabulum, suitable to that large and influential class to which the above-mentioned dictum referred.

TRINITY COLLEGE.
June, 1892.

CHAPTER I.

Trinity College, Dublin.

Monimentum aere perennius.

WHERE Trinity College now rears its gaunt front once stood a priory of the Augustinians, which made the eastern outpost of the city. It was a little city then, clustering about Dublin Castle, and with a tendency to stretch westward rather than east or south, where its prosperities now abide. If one lets his thoughts fly back a few centuries, it is easy to picture the monks in cowl and habit as they prayed and toiled amidst their marshy surroundings, away from the noise of the city—for Westmoreland-street was still far on in the future, and the northern river-banks were lonely marshes, given over to gull and curlew. The one bridge spanning the river was at Essex Gate, and led to the great Abbey of St. Mary, which, with its dependencies, made a little city of itself to the north-west of the river. At the foot of the bridge stood a little squat tower—Izod's Tower—where, they say, La Belle Isonde, of many legends, used to watch for the coming of the messengers from Mark of Cornwall. Another relic of her survives in Chapelizod, beyond Phœnix Park, where her father built a chapel for her soul's sake. But to turn aside from apocrypha to hard facts, the Monastery of All Hallows was sequestrated in due course by Henry VIII., and by him handed over to the Mayor and Corporation of Dublin, as a reward for their help in suppressing the insurrection of Silken Thomas.

Harry's daughter was on the throne before the foundations were laid of the new college, which was to bear the state and title of the College of the Holy and Undivided Trinity. On the application of Archbishop Loftus, the site was granted by the Mayor and Corporation. The laying of the first stone was performed with great ceremony by Thomas Smyth, Mayor of the city, on the 13th March, 1591, and so well was the building pushed forward that the first students were admitted on the 9th of January, 1593.

The buildings of Trinity College have no such mellow age as those of Oxford and Cambridge. None of them dates later than Queen Anne, and there is no fragment of the little square of red Dutch brick which formed the original college. For all that, the place is venerable enough, cobwebby, dusty, worm-eaten, looking at least as ancient as the English universities. Perhaps it presents a somewhat forbidding seriousness of aspect. A visitor would say that by contrast Trinity represents the Protestant genius in architecture, for whatever Protestantism may have done for us intellectually, she has given us little that is artistically beautiful. It is all mathematically arranged, cold and stern and dark. There are none of those quiet grass-grown quads with the graves of the dead under the cloisters, and rose-trees climbing the arches to the low-browed college windows, such as one remembers lovingly at Oxford. If it has kinship with any of its fellows across sea, it is with its namesake at Cambridge, which seems to suggest somewhat similarly the dominance of Christopher Wren and the Protestant austerity.

There are three quads in Trinity College. The front includes Parliament-square—so-called because of the liberal grants given the college by the Irish Parliament for its rebuilding and that of the west front of the college—and the Library-square. These were once divided by a row of buildings, where the Campanile now stands. In one of these buildings Goldsmith is said to have had rooms. The Library-square contains Rotten-row— the oldest buildings in college, some of which were standing in the latter part of the 17th century. The front square has a fine spaciousness, somewhat marred by the hideous waste of uneven pavements in the midst. It has the principal buildings—the Library, under which, until a few years ago, was a grand old cloister, now unhappily built up, to afford greater accommodation for the books and their readers ; the Chapel, gloomy and dark within, with its heavy pews of carved oak, but with a fine window of Munich glass, and steps and chancel-rails of Galway marble, not Carrara, as in many of the Catholic churches in Ireland; the Examination Hall, with its walls covered with portraits, and containing the tomb of Provost Baldwin, while in the gallery stands the famous organ which was taken from the Spaniards in Vigo Bay, 1702, repaired and enlarged by Cuvillie in 1705, and presented to the college by the second Duke of Ormonde; and the Dining Hall, which also contains a number of portraits, including one of Henry Grattan. The new square consists of solid, respectable-looking houses of a very unacademic type, but their ugliness is somewhat atoned for by the beauty of the ancient thorn-trees in the well-kept quadrangle. In May and June the rich bloom of pink and white makes the new square almost beautiful; and the eastern wall is covered with Virginia creepers—thanks to the loving care of Mr. Cathcart, the only one of the Fellows who seems to care for such things. The Museum buildings, ornate out of keeping with the rest of the place, overlook the new square, and, it is said, won the approval of Mr. Ruskin. Botany Bay, the third quadrangle, is popularly held to be the habitation of the wilder spirits, though hard-reading men are as common there as in most other places. At the end of Term, especially, it is the scene of many a festive gathering, and oft-times the stillness of midnight is broken by the cheers which greet the successful lighting of a bonfire, or the cries of "Tally-ho," which announce to the initiated that a cat has been started.

The buildings in the Bay are more than usually hideous, and one longs for a mantle of green ivy to cover their nakedness. A grass plot has of late struggled into existence, but sadly intersected by footpaths. Some time ago a fence of barbed wire was put up, to discourage students from taking short-cuts across the grass, but it was demolished within about an hour of its erection by the indignant inhabitants. Behind the new Square lies the "Wilderness," so called, and to the south stretches the College Park. There it is pleasant to lie in flannels in the summer, and smoke and dream, with three good months of freedom before one, and when the Campanile bell no longer summons to chapel or to the Examination Hall. Very pleasant it is to be away from the noise of the streets, which makes but a dreamy hum in the distance. The place, despite its gloominess of face, has the charm of stillness and seclusion in the heart of a city. The quaint old-world air which belongs to a

University hangs about it, and recalls the Augustinians, their prayers and their labours.

But it is not given to dream too long in the green Wilderness or beneath the trees of the park. One may not pace the walks over long with a chosen friend, dear in that fresh confidence of a college friendship, such as Clough loves to depict. The authorities have so ordained it, that neither Wilderness nor park is allowable at a time when one would enjoy them most. After 6 p.m. in the summer evenings, all day long on a summer Sunday, the gates are locked, and the student may swelter in his dark rooms, and swear at officialism in general and in particular. Even the grass plots of the Front Square are sacred, and one may not lie thereon, or swing on the chains which guard them, without incurring a severe reprimand. They do not cultivate the beautiful in Trinity; and one would look in vain for the window boxes of scarlet geranium and blue lobelia which in summer light up the walls of the English Universities. With its murky low-browed windows, its dusty stairs, its smoke-blackened walls, the old place does not show to advantage, though doubtless it awakens as enthusiastic affections and heart-felt regrets as its more beautiful sisters across the water. Outside the statues of Burke and Goldsmith, by Foley, stand in grassy spaces, which, before the dust of the streets has dimmed their brightness, are sometimes a pleasant sea of daisies. It will strike a new-comer how little the town and the University are for one another; how independent their lives, so strangely unlike Oxford and Cambridge, where the towns seem so entirely made for and dependent upon the Universities. Cap and gown rarely appear outside the walls, except when the students follow the body of some lately-deceased don to its last resting-place. One advantage the separation of town and gown has, is, that Dublin college-men do not walk the streets in fear of meeting a proctor at every corner, for, be it for good or ill, the college dons have no jurisdiction outside their own precincts.

CHAPTER II.

*Le temps s'en va, le temps s'en va, ma dame,
Las! le temps non : mais nous, nous en allons!*

DEAR, indeed, are the years of one's life in this college, even though she be less adorned than other mothers of learning. It is a time when one stands on the very edge of life, eager for a plunge into life's joyous waters, when one has assumed the toga of one's manhood, and is yet a boy in heart. Despite the responsibilities of examinations and lectures, there is a delightful freedom and reckless gaiety in college life, and a *cameraderie* never felt in later years.

To get a set of rooms to yourself, with an outer door for retreat, and a dunscope for inspection of the casual visitor, is to enter at once into one's kingdom of independence. How different it is from the family life shared with many, and how immeasurably removed above the sordid freedom of a life in lodgings! For, at times, even the roughest of us will feel something of the glamour of the old place that has seen the young of so many generations come and tarry and pass away. No one who has not lived within 'varsity walls can understand it, or feel how true are the words of the German poet—

> "Es gibt kein schoener Leben
> Als studentenleben."

Life-long friendships often date from college days, and it is no wonder that it is to those days, and not to one's school-days, our thoughts go back longingly in later life. Every one is not fortunate enough to be accommodated with rooms in college, for although there are forty houses, so much of them is given over to the Fellows and Professors that the room left is only sufficient for about 300 students. But once secured, those brown little rooms are apt to become very dear to one. The furniture varies according to the means and taste of the occupant. Trinity harbours few plutocrats, but some rooms have a fair share of luxury, and most are comfortable, despite the draughts from door and windows and the shower of dust a noisy movement may bring down from wall and ceiling. The generosity of the college supplies one article of furniture—a sort of bookcase-cum-cupboard. The rest the student finds from his own pocket. And so, as in days of dearth, it may chance that half-a-dozen men between them could not furnish forth a single gold coin, the rooms are sometimes ill-plenished. We are a happy medium between the Christ Church man, who may put half his distant inheritance in pawn to Oxford traders for a supply of Ouida-like luxuries, and those students at the democratic Scotch universities, who in one case, according to a famous novelist, rented a bed between three of them, and took each his turn to occupy it. It is, indeed, told of two hard-working brothers in Trinity that they possessed but one small bed between them, wherein one slept while the other read.

One man may have pictures, books, photographs, and fine furniture, while another may be reduced, as was a neighbour of mine, to a square deal table and two broken chairs. He eked out the sitting accommodation, if he had visitors, by his trunks and the coal-box. He satisfied his æsthetic instincts by having on his walls the most comprehensive and highly coloured assortment of pictorial advertisements, and such trophies of illicit enterprise as door-knockers. Over his bedroom door were the printed words, "Third Smoking," which had formerly graced a railway carriage, and, regarded as an indication of the comfort

TRINITY COLLEGE, DUBLIN. 7

A STUDENT'S ROOM.

to be looked for within, were not wholly inapplicable in their present position. The walls of his sitting-room were adorned with such placards as "None but Guinness kept," "All dogs prosecuted; trespassers shot," while on the back of his door was one containing the significant words, "Always on draught." He is gone now, and the place knows him no more; he sleeps beneath the stars of an African sky.

Before the student takes possession of his rooms, he must deposit with the Registrar of chambers a sum of money nearly sufficient to build the whole house. When he is leaving, the rooms are inspected by the Registrar, and the amount of dilapidation caused by himself and his predecessors is deducted from this deposit.

The dunscope is an invention peculiar to Trinity, Dublin.

A DUNSCOPE.

It is a long funnel-like structure, widening out gradually, through which, from its narrow end, the student can get a general view of any individual standing at his door, and so may sport his oak if necessary. The dunscope, delightfully suggestive of the manners of the time it was devised in, exists only in the older houses.

Every room has its tobacco-jar and pipe rack; for the Trinity man, like the German student, is devoted to the divine weed. Musical men add to the regulation furniture a piano, and I heard a lady tell the other day, more prettily than I can, the apotheosis of an old piano. She beheld it first a square, lumbering thing in the high attic of an undergraduate, as poor as happy, as careless as the best of them. When she climbed his stairs of an afternoon to make and dispense his tea for him among a little bevy of damsels, it used to hold a heterogeneous collection of things, and its burden, truth to speak, somewhat deadened the notes the young man drew forth to accompany his song, when he sang for an easily propitiated company, twenty golden years ago. Of the damsels, he loved the fairest—and married her too, despite the frowns of guardians, to whom high hopes and love and pluck were not negotiable things. The next time the narrator saw the old piano was in somewhat poor lodgings, where the young couple were settled, and instead of the things that cumbered it of old, the young wife had decked it in flowers. Years after, when the student had won for himself name and fame, she was talking to the wife in her stately drawingroom in a great square, and commented on the grand Broadwood which stretched across the end of the room. "But what have you done with the old piano?" she asked. "Oh," said the wife, with a smile, "it has the most honoured place in my husband's study. But we never call it old to him. He thinks there never was an instrument like it." Very few college pianos have such an honoured old age. I knew one in Rotten Row which "contrived a double debt to pay." Though its strings were constantly being called into requisition to clean pipes, it never failed when called upon for an accompaniment to a song.

In former days Trinity students had their breakfasts supplied from the Buttery, as at Oxford and Cambridge; but the college authorities, with that zeal for their charges which distinguishes them, conceived the wisdom of turning us out as fit for the Bush by reason of our domestic knowledge, as for the office of Lord Chancellor by reason of our learning.

Trinity men have now to depend on their own skill to poach an egg or grill a beefsteak, and three years' practice in College, when one may be the victim of his own cooking, is worth more

A SKIP.

to him than a wilderness of cookery books. The less dignified offices are performed, or not performed, by individuals who are called skips, a blending of the "gyp" and the "scout" at Oxford and Cambridge.

These skips are usually army pensioners, inordinately proud of having served her Majesty, and of the most perfect inefficiency. They take a holiday at least once a quarter, for three or four days, when they testify their loyalty to her Majesty by vinous celebrations. During these absences the hapless student gains further valuable experience by ministering himself to his own comforts.

The etiquette of skipdom is very strict, and forms a strong contrast to the casual laws that govern intercourse among the students. Never does one skip address another without prefixing his title in polite society. They always have a near and dear relative either just deceased, or on the point of death, and this melancholy circumstance furnishes them with a ready excuse for derelictions of duty.

Most of these Bobadils have in their martial days performed prodigies of valour. An old skip told me that he was within one of getting the Victoria Cross, and when I inquired how, he said he once stood next a man who got it. Wars and rumours of wars are dear unto them, and their language smacks of blood. Their longevity is greater than that of the proverbial crow, and even the influenza, though much was hoped from it, has failed to thin their ranks.

They are, of course, far below the dignity of the College janitors, resplendent in their liveries of dark blue with brass buttons bearing the College arms, and velvet hunting caps. An old chronicler in describing the College says: "On the left side as you enter the vestibule is the porters' lodge, as it is called, and although it is but an humble apartment, and its occupants sober and discreet men, yet its influence is, by a certain class of students, technically known as 'Town Haunters,' considered more depressing and pestiferous than the vapours of Trophonius's cave or those of the celebrated Grotto del Cani. When Great Tom has ceased to toll the hour of nine, this portal is closed, and then vigilance puts into activity her sharpest features, that none may enter without being 'noted down.'"

After chapel on Sunday morning the typical College breakfast is made and eaten. About five guests, who contribute their *sumbola* of viands, together with their host, set about preparing the feast. One man toasts bread, another fries sausages, a third poaches eggs, a fourth makes tea and coffee, and so on, each performing his allotted task. Sometimes they do not work altogether in harmony, and things become a little mixed, but the result is generally satisfactory to the gastronomy of the partakers—for a couple of hours spent in chapel, if not in prayer, is hardly likely to encourage a fastidious appetite. At times ladies, who have attended morning chapel, honour us with their presence at breakfast, which becomes in that case a much more conventional meal.

Dinner in Hall is at 6 p.m. in winter, 6.30 p.m. in summer—a somewhat early hour, but most convenient for reading men, who burn the midnight oil, as well as allowing ample time to catch theatres, concerts, etc.

The Fellows and Fellow-commoners, and of these latter there are but few, dine at a table which stretches across the end of the Hall. They dine better and are seated more comfortably than the ordinary students, on chairs of wondrous softness. For a student to take one of these chairs is regarded by some of the Fellows, at least, as a gross infringement of their prerogatives. In spite of the allurements of soft seats and good dinners I

THE EGG-CUP.

have noticed the Fellow-commoners do not seem very happy; nor is this much to be wondered at when it is considered what a great gulf intellectually exists between them and the dons. The ordinary Students sit on forms at long narrow tables, eat plainer dinners, and drink an attenuated small beer, peculiar to College. According to the opinion of one of the Fellows, the most valuable part of a passman's education is derived from the conversation of the scholars at commons. This is probably an exaggeration, for one notices that the conversationalists most readily listened to are not distinguished from an academic point of view. Before dinner one of ten scholars of blameless lives and exemplary character, appointed for the purpose, and called *waiters*, ascends a pulpit at the right-hand side of the Fellows' table, and repeats *memoriter* the following grace:—"Oculi omnium in te sperant Domine. Tu das iis escam eorum in tempore opportuno. Aperis tu manum tuam et imples omne animal benedictione tua, Miserere nostri te quaesumus Domine tuisque donis quae de tua benignitate sumus percepturi. Benedicito per Christum Dominum nostrum." During dinner the students beguile the time by playing roulette for pennies with a knife set revolving on the bottom of an upturned glass. After dinner the following grace is repeated:—"Tibi laus, tibi honor, tibi gloria, O beata et gloriosa, Trinitas. Sit nomen Domini benedictum et nunc et in perpetuum. Laudamus te benignissime Pater pro serenissimis, Regina Elizabetha hujus Collegii condatrice, Jacobo ejusdem munificentissimo auctore, Carolo conservatore ceterisque benefactoribus nostris. Rogantes te ut his tuis donis recte ad tuam gloriam utentes in hoc seculo, te una cum fidelibus in futurum feliciter perfruamur per Christum Dominum nostrum."

If a student be seen talking during grace he is liable to be sharply rebuked by one of the Junior Fellows, whose learning is only equalled by their piety and godliness.

The etiquette of College life is peculiar. Instead of the formal call, as at Oxford, a kick at the door, and a request for the "loan" of tea, coffee, &c., with the invitation to share them, often break the ice between the new-comer and his neighbour. Indeed, the property of men living in the same house is generally regarded as common, and only the very greenest "jib" would be guilty of such a breach of etiquette as restoring borrowed articles of food, the characters of lender and borrower being so easily interchanged.

CHAPTER III.

If sack and sugar be a fault, God help the wicked.

THE youthful aspirant to the honours of gown and mortar-board will, if he be well-advised, pick out the tutor who is reported to excel in the Socratic virtue of being able to make the worse appear the better reason; in other words,

> "To change the nought into
> The three that lets all duffers through."

Occasionally misconceptions as to the tutorial function have occurred. Some little time ago a pupil wrote to his tutor telling him that he was engaged during the day, and asking him if it would be sufficient to come to him for instruction five evenings of the week. The answer he received was not quite what he expected. Another pupil during the "Long" sent from the country a weekly budget to his tutor, containing an account not only of his own doings, but also of those of his family, and wound up by saying that his sisters sent their love. Whether this latter was regarded as an extenuating circumstance or not, I don't know, but certain I am that such pupils are not appreciated by their tutors as, perhaps, they deserve.

In College one belongs to one's year and makes friends and comrades of one's contemporaries. Every year the old place is filled with new faces, so that a lingerer past the conventional time is apt to feel somewhat *désolé*, as though his youth had passed away with his first years.

It is not advisable to incur dislike in old Trinity. A few years ago there was an outbreak of popular feeling against a man who had been the means of getting two fellow-students rusticated. He knew no peace. His windows were broken, his door screwed up, and whenever he succeeded in getting out he was saluted with a fusillade of coal from the windows. Then one night three students, with blackened faces, lay in wait for him on the staircase, and as he was ascending to his rooms they threw a gown over his head, tied him down, and cut off one side of his moustache, of which he was particularly proud. Finally, his rooms were broken into one night when he was absent, and his furniture smashed and burned. Then he accepted the inevitable, and removed his hated presence from the College.

A man may, however, be very popular without possessing any very exalted virtues. Such a one was genial, devil-may-care, impecunious Paddy Branagan, and stories about him are still passed delightedly from mouth to mouth, stories not always retailable in prudish society. He was, indeed, the Falstaff of Trinity, and in person he bore no slight resemblance to his great prototype. When I knew him he was "a good portly man and a corpulent, of a cheerful look, a pleasing eye, and a most noble carriage." In his undergraduate days, and they were many, for it was no part of his ambition to excel at exams., he was the darling and delight of all the sportsmen in College. No spree was a success without Paddy, and when one saw his rubicund visage and portly figure, one felt it was good to be there. His jokes were as brilliant as his tales were inexhaustible. In giving nicknames he was very happy, and they always clung to a man, as, for instance, when he dubbed a candidate, who had gone up many times for Scholarship, "the hardy annual." He sang, too, "certainly with other notes than to the Orphean lyre," but he had a peculiar style of his own, perfectly inimitable. His favourite song was the "Last Rose of Summer," which he sang in falsetto; he could play one waltz, and always did at a spree, if there was a piano and the night was far spent. His speeches, too, were wonderful, and he was so carried away by his feelings that he nearly always required support before he came to the peroration. He sometimes came into collision with the authorities, but his ready wit and blarney almost invariably saved him when he failed to establish the justice of his case. In his freshman year he took rooms above the Dean's, and the first article of furniture introduced was a barrel of stout. Owing to his many visitors this did not long escape the Argus eye of the Dean. He sent for Paddy, and rebuked him for commencing his academical career in this wise. The culprit, unabashed, replied that he had been ordered stout by the doctor, and, as a proof of the good it had done him already, he said that at first he was unable even to move the barrel, but now he could roll it round the room with ease. Most College men will remember his reply to a question in logic on the illicit moods—I O U *non valet*. He paid rather dearly for this joke, for the examiner told him he was not only ignorant but insolent, and gave him 0. After he ceased to reside in College, and had been called to the Bar, he had a chequered career. He quarrelled many times with his father, who did not always approve of his son's conduct, and then the supplies were cut off. During these periods Paddy called himself an orphan, and being often *in extremis*, railed against paternal ingratitude.

His substantial form was rarely absent from the smoking-room of the " Phil.," *i.e.*, the Philosophical, the younger of the College's two debating societies, where, surrounded by a goodly company, he cracked his jokes from noon till night. He was reported to lodge occasionally in the " Phil.," and one night as he was leaving College much after hours the usual question was put to him by the janitor: " Whose rooms do you come from, sir ? " " From the ' Phil.,' " was the reply. " But," objected the porter, " they turn out the gas there at twelve o'clock." " Bedad, then, they didn't turn me out, anyhow," retorted the irrepressible Paddy.

His wit and repartee were spontaneous and begotten of the moment, but he was rarely persuaded to put anything on paper. He did, however, write a play, in which he dramatised his more intimate friends, the scene whereof was laid in " the wineshop of one Corlesius," and he invented a new " Rake's Progress." Unfortunately most of his jokes must be classed as *nefanda*.

The last time I saw Paddy was at the railway station in Tralee. I asked him how he was. " High in spirits, but low in purse," he replied, and, putting his hand in his pocket, he pulled out a few coppers. He had just taken a third-class ticket to his native city, and it and the coppers represented all that was left of his earnings on circuit. Shortly afterwards he disappeared, none knew whither, and we mourned him as one dead. But a little while ago he reappeared as a flourishing burgher in one of New England's mighty cities. The local papers were full of his praises, and he bade fair to become as famous there as he had been here, but in a different way. We read and marvelled, feeling all the while the poorer for his loss, and owning sadly we "ne'er shall see his like again."

Hardly inferior to Paddy Branagan was merry, ruddy-visaged Charlie Burke. His laugh was the most infectious I ever heard, and by means of it and his brogue, for he hailed from Galway, he earned the reputation of a wit; and, I believe, he thought (as honestly as he could) himself to be one. Anyhow it was cheaply earned, for he had only to say *Bedad* or *Begorra* to set a whole table on a roar. He was the best-natured fellow I ever met, and you could get anything out of him except the truth, but those who knew him well never expected that from him. When in the country, it was said, he spent his time concocting adventures in which, of course, he himself played a prominent part. But these tales were no amateurish ones, for he never made himself out a hero, so that they might more readily gain credence, as they often did. The rôle he played was often ridiculous, never sublime. It was impossible to "score off" him for he joined in most heartily when the laugh was against himself. Under certain circumstances he gave expression to the most exalted sentiments, and the beauty of his language in praise of virtue and truth were only surpassed by his fiery denunciations of vice and falsehood. If he told the truth, and sometimes he did by accident, a little persuasion added to the antecedent improbability of his so doing, would convince him afterwards of its falsity.

It was my good fortune to go on several cycling tours with him, and a merrier companion (if the day was fine) I never found. He made friends with whomsoever he met, in village or by the roadside, and for every pretty girl he had a pretty speech ready, which almost invariably ended the conquest his "purty" face and bright blue eyes had begun. I often envied him his glibness, for he always anticipated what my halting tongue would fain say, yet I forgave him when I shared the comforts and good things which his winning ways procured. After a few ineffectual struggles I began to submit to be regarded as a sort of appendage of his, and being constantly referred to as "your friend" ceased to trouble me. Only when he heard a dog bark far on in the road, could I assert myself and take precedence of him; the bark of a dog, he said, jarred on his nerves.

When we were taking our leave of town or village, all the maidens, fair and otherwise, would come to see us off, and fling "God speeds" after us. I have said I never found a merrier travelling companion if the day was fine; if it was wet, then no such matter. He would talk dismally on all the ills which the flesh is heir to, beginning with lumbago, and ending with consumption, unless happily a glass of punch intervened. Once I saw him non-plussed, and my heart was glad thereat. Two fair damsels were discussing him. One said, "He's a fine man, God bless him." "Yes," retorted the other, "if he was any finer there'd be nothin' of him at all." Charlie, indeed, could not without exaggeration be called burly, and he told me the same night that the reason of his slightness was, his heart was too big for his body. One evening we were dining together at a country hotel in the north of Ireland. Opposite us sat a mild, nervous-looking man, who every now and then gazed with furtive suspicion at Charlie's beaming face. At last he leaned over to Charlie and asked—"Are you in boots?" "Yes, of course I am," was the reply. "How long?" asked the stranger, in tones almost despairing. "Almost since I could carry them," said Charlie, laughing. The stranger heaved a deep sigh, rose from the table, and abruptly left the room. Next morning we inquired of him, and learned that he had left the hotel in the small hours of the morning. He was, we discovered later, a traveller in the boot-trade, and evidently feared Charlie would anticipate his orders.

During his collegiate days he founded a club, now unhappily extinct, called the "Corks." He himself presided, under the euphonious title of "The Lord High Bung," and held the power of excluding from membership any candidate with whose claims he was dissatisfied. The meeting place of the "Corks" was in Charlie's rooms, and there abundance of stout, beer, and whiskey were stored, to be had for phenomenally cheap prices. On the wall hung a scroll containing the price list; on a small table, at one of the windows, stood a money-box, into which the members dropped the price of their draught, or else marked it and their names on a slate, which was attached to the back of the door: for the "Corks" were, or were supposed to be, all honourable men. Once a month a general meeting was held, the accounts of the society were audited, and a statement made of the profit and loss. The proceedings at each of these meetings were inserted in a minute-book. When Charlie was leaving college he resigned the office of "Lord High Bung," and advertised an auction of his effects, the intrinsic value of which was about five shillings, for the meetings of the "Corks" in his rooms did not tend to enhance the worth of his furniture. However, Charlie put a placard on his window, with "Stout for Purchasers" inscribed thereon. The bait took; on the day of the auction the rooms were crowded. Charlie acted as auctioneer, and the bidding was so keen that he found himself in possession of nine pounds clear at the end of the sale. After Charlie left college, the *morale* of the members of the society seemed to deteriorate, and though it lingered on for a while longer, it became finally extinct.

I have spoken of him in the past tense. The old Charlie exists no longer; the once roving eye roves no more, but is quiet as a nun's; though the hand-grasp is as firm, and the voice as mellow as ever, the smile is slower than of yore, and every year a "little one" adds a wrinkle to his brow. Soon, I fear, he may even decline into veracity, and then his fame will perish in oblivion.

If Trinity has up to the present no Calverly she has produced in Edwin Hamilton a humorist of whom any University might be proud. In his undergraduate days he won the Vice-Chancellor's Prize in English Verse for a humorous poem on Ariadne, and since, he has published the well known "Dublin Doggerels" and "The Moderate Man."

Mr. Hamilton has kindly allowed me to publish a few specimens of the original stanza of his "Faust" as recited in College rooms, at club dinners, &c.

"Behold," said Meph, "the lovely Marguerite,"
And he showed her in a vision, sitting spinning on a seat.
    Her hair in plaits hung down,
    Slate-blue her simple gown,
        For "neat
Not gaudy" was the motto of the lovely Marguerite.

      *   *   *

Then the antiquated physiologist,
By a turn of Mephistopheles' rejuvenating wrist,
    Became a youth, nor could
    A girl, however good,
        Resist
The handsome reinvigorated physiologist.

      *   *   *

As the warrior appeared upon the scene,
Faust whispered to the tempter (who remarked him looking green
    "It's just as well, you know,
    To have a friend or so
      Between,
When infuriated warriors appear upon the scene."

       *   *   *

Mephistopheles then flourished in the air
A paper, showing traces of combustion here and there ;
    The Doctor, looking wild,
    Said, "I never from a child
      Could bear
To see a fellow flourishing a paper in the air."

Mr. William Wilkins is one of the few Trinity men who have celebrated their *alma mater* in verse.

The following stanzas I take from his poem on T.C.D.

Up here I sleep in the hawthorn scent,
  It swims through my windows from lawn to lawn,
While June's first nights with their deep content,
  Possess my spirit from dusk to dawn.

       *   *   *

Eastward, westward, spread in the dark,
  An acre of grass, an acre of daisies ;
Northward, a square ; to the south, a park ;
  Mine is the midmost of pleasant places.

Hence I can see, as the midnight wears,
  The first blue tides of the morning steal
Between shores of cloud, among fleets of stars,
  Blanching the coigns of the Campanile,

And all the divine repose that looms
  Through the College courts as the sweet hours go ;
Palatial piles and their cloistered glooms,
  And dormer, and terrace, and portico.

       *   *   *

And so I sleep in the hawthorn scent,
  That dwells with me here like a haunting passion,
And so in the city I wait content,
  While the time draws on to the long vacation.

CHAPTER IV.

*Grau, theurer Freund, ist alle Theorie
Und grün des Lebens goldner Baum.*

THE Exams. are naturally the most irksome part of College life. Sometimes an unholy alliance is entered into between the Classical and Mathematical men on a reciprocal basis. The best place for carrying out an arrangement of this kind is behind the monument of Provost Baldwin in the Examination Hall, where one is not seen from the dais on which the examiners sit. A College superstition is that it is very unlucky for a candidate to sit under the portrait of Queen Elizabeth, which hangs on the wall facing the Provost's tomb. That the art of cribbing is not yet obsolete may be inferred from the following story. A *viva voce* Exam. in physics was held in the Engineering School, and the examiner noticed that as each successive candidate presented himself, the answering showed a continuous improvement. Perceiving that they had communicated the questions to one another, he determined to prevent it effectually in future. On the next occasion he shut the candidates up in a room, and sent for the examinees one by one. To his surprise the same thing happened as before, for the first men barely got passmarks and the last answered everything. The explanation was simple. The first to be examined looked out the numbers of the page and section in Ganot's Physics, where the questions were explained, and telegraphed them by means of the cricket telegraph board in the park to their imprisoned comrades.

The relations between classical men and mathematical men in College are an interesting confirmation of the truth of the old proverb—*pares cum paribus facillume congregantur*, for one rarely finds them consorting together. Reading men indulge in the mild dissipation of a game of whist after the post-prandial tea and are rarely to be found among those who after commons adjourn to "the Bay" to try their luck at *motty* or pitch and toss. An ancient statute of the College forbade those under the standing of M.A. to play marbles on the dining-hall steps, as well as to shoot snipe in the Park.

Trinity is a good foster-mother of vigorous sons, and athletics flourish here more than anywhere else in Ireland. There is much friendly rivalry between the various clubs, but the most general consent gives the palm to the football club, which last season established the reputation of Dublin University as the premier Varsity in football, by defeating the representatives of both Oxford and Cambridge. Lacrosse has been recently revived in Trinity and bids fair to become very popular.

One of the laws of the place is against the admittance of dogs to College. A student may neither keep the friend of man himself, nor may he stroll in casually in the wake of a visitor. How different from Oxford, where one may see in summer weather men in many coloured blazers strolling down to Salter's, each with half-a-dozen bull pups at his heels. And yet we are often reminded of the advantages which we possess over those enjoyed by English University men. A little while ago an audacious ex-College man entered by the gate in the Nassau-st. wall, a sacred gate reserved for the Fellows, and of which he somehow possessed a key. Not only this, but a pair of much pampered Dachshunds followed at his heels. When he had entered beyond retreat, he was confronted by the stony horror of the most irascible Fellow in College, who stood with frowning brow at the infringement of two sacred rules. "May I ask, sir," he at length found composure to say, "how it is you come through that gate, and also what you mean by bringing your dogs with you?" "Sir," replied the delinquent meekly, "I found the gate open and knew no rule against coming this way. As for the dogs, they are two curs who have followed me." And he turned therewith and stoned his two beloved Dachshunds, who, paralysed at first by this incomprehensible treatment, finally fled with cries of terrified reproach.

There is a piece of doggerel, highly popular in College, which recounts the adventures of a pair of forlorn "jibs" who failed to pass the Little-go. Its popularity must be my excuse for appending it here:—

MANY A TIME.

About six months ago, perhaps, at the beginning of the year,
My old chum Spifkins said to me "I do begin to fear
That we've not passed the Little-go—our chance looks mighty queer;
Our marks in classics are too bad—they're not the total near.
And as for mathematics, now, you know we didn't do
One quarter of the blessed three which passes scrapers through."
He was quite right, the lists came out, our names we could not see,
But all the same we said we would go out upon the spree.

   For we'd been that way before,
    Many a time, many a time;
    We'd been that way before, many a time;
   In mechanics his marks were a total of 3;
    But 1 was the highest of mine;
   For we'd both been there before,
    Many a time, many a time.

So after Commons that very night, we mustered in the Bay;
We lit a great big bonfire there, with other freshmen gay.
For we knew we'd have some time to spare before we'd supplement,
And the interval we thought would be in rowdiness well-spent.
So we danced about the fire and howled, smashed windows, horns blew;
For often thus we *read* at night; we thrashed a porter too.
At last the night-watch, Jones, appeared with help upon the scene;
He and three porters dragged us both before the Junior Dean.

   We'd both been there before
    Many a time, many a time,
    We'd both been there before, many a time;
   And both of us thought we'd lose our rooms,
    And not without reason or rhyme,
   For we'd both been there before
    Many a time, many a time.

The J. D. said, "Now, what's all this? I told you two before
That if you were brought to me again I'd let you off no more;
You throw more bread than all the rest who dine within the Hall;
At Chapel I've caught you 'putting in,' and climbing o'er the wall;
To-morrow you go before the Board; don't talk now it's no use;
You've talked me down too often now, so please keep your excuse."
He banged the door and shut us out, a luckless pair of "jibs,"
For this time we knew we couldn't well get off by telling fibs.

> For we'd told so many before
>   Many a time, many a time,
>   For we'd told so many before many a time;
> And indignant assertions of innocence, too,
>   With the porter's black eyes wouldn't chime,
> For we'd told so many before
>   Many a time, many a time.

The Board heard all the facts, then our tutors both did fight
To save us rustication, which the Dean said would be right;
A two pound fine was all we got; we bore the loss with ease,
For pater stumps for all of such, under the names of fees.
"Now," said the chum, "we have not paid for this scrape much too dear;
Come with me to some near pub, I'll stand a bitter beer."
We went out to the Burlington and ordered bitter beer.
And all the fellows said we would have better luck next year.

> We'd both been there before
>   Many a time, many a time,
>   We'd both been there before many a time;
> And many a bottle of bitter we'd drunk,
>   And Jameson's old and prime,
> For we'd both been there before
>   Many a time, many a time.

We then stood drinks all round, and tho' I really cannot quite
Explain the reason, all of us appeared to be well tight;
One of the worst—he looked, indeed, a decent sort of chap—
Said, "Let's go back to College and we'll have a game of nap;"
We lost, of course, we always do, and when we'd nothing more,
The others said that they would read, and bowed us to the door;
We'd spent a fiver since we left the rooms that bally morn,
So behind the Bank we went and put our tickers into pawn.

> They'd both been there before
>   Many a time, many a time,
>   They'd both been there before many a time!
> The chum raised a couple of figures on his,
>   But only a dollar on mine,
> And they'd both been there before
>   Many a time, many a time.

And now, said chum, the evening's come, let's look a bit alive,
I won't go in until we blow this blessed two pound five;
A box at Daniel Lowrey's next, to drink and smoke and shout,
As each performer pleased us more, until they chucked us out;
A supper at the Dolphin, then; what next I cannot tell,
For I awoke next morning feeling bad with a headache in a cell.
Old K——ys said, "Twenty bob and costs, or the treadmill you must tread,"
I said "We're students; let us off." He looked at us and said:

"You've both been here before
　Many a time, many a time,
　You've both been here before many a time ;
To gentlemen rowdies in future I'll not
　Give even the option of fine,
For you've both been here before
　Many a time, many a time."

For the information of the uninitiated it may be mentioned that by the expression "putting in" an ancient and time-honoured custom is referred to, whereby a student may seem to be in Chapel, whilst lying quietly in bed he enjoys "the honey heavy dew of slumber."

CHAPTER V.

Socii cratera coronant.

SPREES, which are usually given to celebrate an event, such as the winning of scholarship, or passing the Little-go, or the failure to do either of these things, play an important part in College life. The last week of Term there is generally an embarrassment of riches in the way of sprees. The spree is not conducted on total abstinence principles, as may be gathered from the following card of invitation:—

43, Trinity College.

DEAR SIR,—A movement having been inaugurated for the purpose of putting down drink, a meeting of its supporters will be held on Saturday next in the above rooms at nine o'clock p.m. You are requested by attendance to show your interest in this absorbing question, and we hope at the close of the meeting to be in a position to exhibit some examples of the baneful effects of intemperance.—Yours truly,

JOSIAH SNOOKS.

A temperance magazine got hold of this joke, and published it shortly afterwards as a proof of the wickedness of College men.

The drinks, which consist of champagne (if the occasion be an important one), whiskey, stout, beer, &c., are supplied by the host; the additional glasses, chairs, and other conveniences necessary, by such of his friends as possess them. The guests begin to drop in soon after Commons, but it is 10 o'clock before the symposium is in full swing. There is less formality about the *spree* than there is about the Oxford *wine* or the German *Kneipe*, but it possesses some of the characteristics of both. After the health of the host is proposed and responded to, speeches in praise of *Wein und Weib*, often delivered in the manner of some well-known Fellow; songs, racy stories full of point, if somewhat lacking in delicacy, follow one another in

A COLLEGE SPREE.

quick succession. The fun, noise, and laughter wax furious, until as the dawn begins to creep slowly in through the windows one hears—

"From grammar defiers,
Long constructions, strange and plusquam Thucydidean,"

as the bibulous orators stagger

"All through sentences, six at a time, unsuspecting of Syntax."

It sometimes happens that the party is surprised by an unwelcome visitor, in the person of the Junior Dean, who enters accompanied by two janitors. In this case the J. D. delivers the concluding oration, which is couched in language far from complimentary to the host, and frequently ends with an invitation to be present at the next "At Home" given by the Board. The following verses, written by an old *spree boy*, and affectionately dedicated to his former attic dwelling, may give some notion of a spree:—

> Wisha, sweet twenty-seven,
> You're as high up as heaven,
>   Tho' the door to poor sinners is free;
> For a scholar elected, or passman rejected,
>   'Tis there was the place for a spree.
>
> Oh! the first was champagne,
> Soon there's left not a drain,
>   But the whiskey flows on and flows free
> Like a stream; and within is
> A cartload of Guinness,
>   The staple of Grandison's spree.
>
> Then the toasts and the songs,
> Keeping time with the tongs,
>   'Till the noctivigating J. D.
> In the doorway appears;
> He's received with three cheers
>   By the bold boys at Grandison's spree.
>
> Down in less than a wink went
> The list of delinquent
>   Who figured at that night's levee;
> Cries of speech from the Dean
> Follow off from the scene
>   A guest never asked to the spree.
>
> Oh! to see Johnny Moore
> When he's full take the floor
>   In the midst of the devil's *debris*,
> 'Till with gesticulating
> He falls still orating,
>   'Mid the plaudits of Grandison's spree.
>
> Fin is stretched by the fender,
> The last to surrender;
>   On the lounge is unconscious Magee.
> There's a crash on the lobby,
> 'Tis little M'Robbie
>   Departing from Grandison's spree.
>
> The rest slide and tumble
> Downstairs—a grand jumble,
>   While all in being sober agree,
> "Old man, I'm all right,"
> Is the parting good night
>   On the morning of Grandison's spree.

Another event of the summer season is the College Races, to Trinity what the May races are to Cambridge. Most of the students' friends and relatives come to town for this social event, and enjoy the novelty of being entertained in College rooms. When the day is fine, and of late years this has happened but seldom, the park and quads are filled with fair women in gay coloured frocks—something for the hapless student who spends his vac. in Trinity to dream of when College is as a city of the dead, and the desolation is greater than the desolation of Balclutha. College Races night is generally spent by the gayer young bloods at the circus in wild enjoyment, which sometimes leads to the police-court next morning. The graver ones are content to rest after a day well spent in dispensing tea and coffee, fruit and claret-cup. There used to be two days of the College Races, but an outbreak of wild spirits, which made the gay youth select the College carpenter's workshop as material for a bonfire, caused the races to be suspended for several years. Their subsequent revival is due to the late Provost, Dr. Jellett, who removed the ban laid on them by his predecessor, but now they are only a one day event.

A few years ago it was the custom to light a bonfire in the middle of Botany Bay, but, owing to the vigilance of the Dean and his myrmidons, this is now of very rare occurrence. I remember once being concerned in such an adventure. Some half-dozen of us during the last days of Term had adjourned to a room in the Bay to play cards, and after a few hours, growing tired of the game, one of us suggested a bonfire. The suggestion was hailed with delight, but the initial difficulty was where to procure the material. After much cogitation we finally decided on casting lots as to who should sacrifice the mattress of his bed, it being agreed that he on whom the lot fell should have immunity from all other responsibility in the matter. Having stationed a man at each corner of the quad to keep watch, we carried the mattress out and put it in the middle of the grass plot, poured a can of paraffin oil on it, set fire to it, and fled. In a few seconds the whole place was illuminated. Every window in the Bay was crowded with delighted spectators, who jeered at the futile attempts of the night watchmen to extinguish the flames. Nemesis was, however, on our track, for all that was left of the mattress was a label bearing the name of its

JENKINS ADDRESSES HIS CONSTITUENTS.

owner, who was duly summoned before the J. D. next day. Fortunately, he was able before his trial, to consult with his colleagues, and decide upon a plausible explanation, which satisfied the Dean, and he was dismissed, with a reprimand.

Anything likely to give occasion for a joke is eagerly welcomed by college men. A little while ago, when it was rumoured that a contested election was likely to take place in Trinity, some undergrads induced one of their number, a somewhat vain and weak-minded individual named Jenkins, to become an aspirant to parliamentary honours. After Commons, they carried him down to the Bay, where he addressed his constituents, promising to procure for them all the reforms which they desired, such as good beer and stout at Commons, abolition of the Board, night roll and fines, except for the cook and porters, and many

other changes tending to the amelioration of their condition. The proceedings were very enthusiastic, and after each public meeting an adjournment was made by the candidate and a few choice spirits who constituted his committee, to his rooms, where his health and future success were drunk amidst loud cheers. One night they carried him out to College Green and set him on King William's statue, where he orated until the "Metropolitans" ordered him to "move on." As he was by this time incapable of any exercise of volition, two of his supporters got him on their shoulders and carried him back to college, where he continued his oration under the clock in the Front Square.

In the middle of an eloquent peroration, a cry of "The Dean" was heard, and a general stampede followed, the luckless candidate being left sprawling on his back, unable to adopt his constituents' motto of *Sauve qui peut*. That was the last incident of his canvass, and whether he still dreams of a seat in the *curia* I know not. In college life he exists now but as a name, "like Henry Pimpernell and old John Naps of Greece."

CHAPTER VI.

E coelo descendit γνῶθι σεαυτὸν.

THE Fellows exercise but little influence on the college life of the student except in their capacity as examiners. In the Exam. Hall they meet "as victim and as executioner," and consequently the relations between them are often somewhat strained. There is little or no social intercourse between them and the students, to whose intellectual level they rarely deign to descend. They give no entertainments to the students like their *confrères* at Oxford and Cambridge. The professorial gown seems always to cling to them, and the majesty of their high position is ever before their eyes. No wonder the undergrads regard them with fear and trembling. As might be expected, they are very conservative, especially the Senior Fellows, and view with grave suspicion any suggestion of reform.

Dr. Salmon, the Provost, to whom Dublin University owes so much of her mathematical reputation, if he know but little of the doings and sufferings of the students, is a genial, kindly man, much given to absent-mindedness. When one meets him in the street he always seems to be chuckling over some new scientific *crux*, which his fertile brain has discovered for the increase of human perplexity. It is reported that he once collided with a cow in a public thoroughfare. He apologised profusely, only discovering his mistake when his apologies were not accepted. A little while after, resentment still fresh in his mind, *nescio quid meditans*, he jostled a lady. "Is it you again, you brute!" cried the irate Provost, and walked quickly on.

C.

He is a famous chessplayer, and used always to play and beat the winner in the College Chess Competition. Once, however,

THE PROVOST.

his record was broken, and now he plays no more. He is passionately fond of music, of which he is no mean critic.

Dr. Carson and Dr. Stack are an old-established and lasting institution in Trinity College. Dr. Carson reads Thucydides by day and dreams of him by night. His perverted ingenuity has devised a book of questions which no man can answer. Dr. Stack's courteous and sympathetic treatment will be gratefully remembered by all scholarship candidates.

Dr. Ingram, the Senior Lecturer, is best known as the author of the following poem on the disastrous movement of

1798, which is justly regarded as the finest and most truly national ballad which Ireland has produced:—

THE MEMORY OF THE DEAD.

Who fears to speak of Ninety-eight?
    Who blushes at the name?
When cowards mock the patriots' fate,
    Who hangs his head for shame?
He's all a knave or half a slave
    Who slights his country thus;
But a *true* man, like you, man,
    Will fill your glass with us.

We drink the memory of the brave,
    The faithful and the few—
Some lie far off beyond the wave,
    Some sleep in Ireland, too;
All, all are gone—but still lives on
    The fame of those who died;
All true men, like you, men,
    Remember them with pride.

Some on the shores of distant lands
    Their weary hearts have laid,
And by the stranger's heedless hands
    Their lonely graves were made;
But, though their clay be far away
    Beyond the Atlantic foam,
In true men, like you, men,
    Their spirit's still at home.

The dust of some is Irish earth;
    Among their own they rest;
And the same land that gave them birth
    Has caught them to her breast;
And we will pray that from their clay
    Full many a race may start
Of true men, like you, men,
    To act as brave a part.

They rose in dark and evil days
    To right their native land;
They kindled here a living blaze
    That nothing shall withstand.
Alas! that Might can vanquish Right—
    They fell, and passed away;
But true men, like you, men,
    Are plenty here to-day.

Then here's their memory—may it be
    For us a guiding light,
To cheer our strife for liberty,
    And teach us to unite!

> Through good and ill, be Ireland's still,
> Though sad as theirs your fate ;
> And true men, be you, men,
> Like those of Ninety-eight.

Dr. Ingram is the *beau ideal* of a classical examiner, and as an elegant scholar he is well known on both sides of the channel. He has lately been elected President of the Royal Irish Academy. Dr. Shaw, the latest acquisition to the ranks of the Senior Fellows, is the wittiest man in College. For an after-dinner speech or a slashing newspaper article he is unrivalled. His lectures, before he " entered into rest " as a Senior Fellow, were as entertaining as his examination questions were eccentric. As an example of the latter two of his questions in Astronomy may be given :—" How do you learn astronomy by going to the theatre ?" Answer expected—" By observation of the stars." " How do you know when the moon is on the wax or the wane ?', "When she's on the wax she's all right, but when she's on the wane its all that's left of her."

DR. HAUGHTON.

Most Dublin people are familiar with the handsome face of Dr. Haughton, though it is seen seldomer in College than of old. Before many of the present men of Trinity had won their spurs, Dr. Haughton was well known as a scholar, scientist, physician, preacher, and, above all, a witty platform speaker. He has long since atoned for the iniquity of the "Manuals," which he perpetrated in conjunction with the late Mr. Galbraith. As an after-dinner anecdotist he divides the honours with Dr. Tisdall, for whom he is said to have an almost fraternal affection.

"THE GENERAL."

Dr. Mahaffy is the *arbiter elegantiarum* of Trinity, and ill betide that man who has the misfortune to appear before him with a soiled collar or necktie awry. Time would fail me were I to attempt to enumerate his many accomplishments. Besides being a historian, linguist, musician, metaphysician, he is a voluminous writer on many subjects from Greek Literature to Table Talk. His lectures are more interesting even than his books. Like his greater countryman, Moore, " he dearly loves a lord," and he includes in the list of his acquaintances many crowned heads. Indeed, it is said that in Greece he is hardly second to the king himself, though, I have heard, the monks of Athos bear him no great love. Many are the stories told of him, some I may not repeat, but others perhaps I may :—One day a lady met him in the College park at a cricket match dressed in a light tweed suit. Astonished, she said—" Oh, Mr. Mahaffy, I thought you were a clergyman !" " A little," replied the Rev. Dr. A member of the Salvation Army, when travelling with him in a railway carriage, asked him was he " saved !" " Yes," was the reply, " but I may tell you in confidence it was a very narrow squeak, and I don't like talking much about it."

THE J. D.

The " General," as he is not inappropriately called, is something of a sportsman, and can still handle the bat better than many a youngster. He is a sort of viceregal *quatorzième*, and his wit often enlivens the dinner-parties of the Viceroy, be he Liberal or Conservative. The caricature sketch given of him was done by a Trinity man some years ago, and represents him in a familiar attitude explaining, as only he can, some knotty problem.

But the most important, and sometimes most formidable of the dons, is Mr. Gray, the Junior Dean. His energy in suppressing bonfires and "larks" is wonderful. During Term he is always on the warpath, and when he sleeps is a mystery to everyone. Being the *censor morum* of College he has often disagreeable duties to perform, but withal he is very popular; and great was the dissatisfaction amongst students when it was rumoured some time ago that a new Junior Dean was to be appointed. Though he is hot-tempered, and in anger gives short shrift, he is very generous and kind-hearted, and not a few students of Trinity have owed their success to his timely aid. Apart from his official qualities, he is an excellent judge of cattle, and can always distinguish beef from horseflesh when the question arises at commons.

Dr. Tyrrell, the Regius Professor of Greek, is the handsomest of the Fellows. He is always courteous, even to an undergrad, preferring to teach good manners by example rather than precept, and few men have attended his lectures without carrying away something at least of his refinement. He fully realises one's notion of an ideal classical scholar, and if his great work on "The Correspondence of Cicero" has brought many a student to the verge of despair, the thought of the fame it has won for Dublin in the classical world has not failed to comfort them.

Dr. Palmer, Professor of Latin and Editor of Horace, Propertius, and Plautus, has added more to the melancholy list of *variae lectiones* than, perhaps, any man living. It is told of him that he asked a candidate what was the best emendation in Catullus, and when he replied, that there might be a difference of opinion about it, the professor exclaimed, "But, sir, *I* have stated in print what is the best emendation." He brooks no contradiction, and the hard pronunciation of a Latin C never fails to rouse his ire. He is, nevertheless, a fair-minded and honourable gentleman, and Trinity would be all the better of a few more like him.

DR. TYRRELL, REGIUS PROFESSOR OF GREEK.

Most indefatigable in his pupils' cause is Dr. Traill, otherwise known as "Tony." He combines physical with intellectual accomplishments. He is a good shot, can ride well, and looks

"TONY."

as though he would prove a very Entellus with his fists. He used to be one of the best racket players in College.

Mr. Cathcart is, perhaps, of all men most terrible to the examinee. He impresses one strongly with an idea of his physical force, and when the candidate takes his seat trembling before him, all the miserable tips, gleaned with infinite pains from the grinder, take unto themselves wings and flee away from his distracted brain. Once he gave me a *post mortem* exam. in astronomy, and one of his questions was—"If you were on a raft in mid-ocean on a clear night how would a knowledge of astronomy teach you your position?" I did not dare to tell him that under those circumstances I should know my position, only too well, without the aid of astronomy; and the answer I did venture to give he characterised as utter nonsense.

In private he is the best of good Fellows and a delightful companion. He is passionately fond of flowers, and to him Trinity owes what little she has in the way of floral beauty.

Mr. Bury, who has lately edited the Nemean and Isthmian Odes of Pindar, is one of the youngest of the Fellows, and looks at least ten years younger than he is. Many stories are told of misguided youths who, deceived by his boyish appearance in the Exam. Hall, imparted to him the secrets of their hearts in respect to certain passages which they had not read, and only discovered their mistake when Mr. Bury sent for them and requested them to construe these particular passages.

Mr. Bury edits *Kottabos*, the College Monthly Magazine, which, during the editorship of Dr. Tyrrell, attained such celebrity

Dr. Dowden, Professor of English Literature, in appearance recalls the features which Vandyke so loved to paint. He has a handsome, dreamy face, with pointed beard, and a soft, somewhat melancholy voice. He is surrounded by a little coterie of literary and would-be literary people, from the youth who has just discovered that some difference exists between the style of Mathew Arnold and that of Robert Browning, to the enthusiast who sought inspiration by spending a night on the tomb of Wordsworth. Yet to each and all he is affable and sympathetic, and can easily come down to the intelligence of his company. By his admirers he is regarded with an almost idolatrous affection. He can speak well, too, though his speeches are somewhat redolent of the lamp.

There are two Fellows in Trinity of whom I have never heard a word but praise—Mr. Louis Claude Purser and Mr. John Isaac Beare. Dr. Atkinson is the Mezzofanti of Trinity and was reputed to know all languages until a letter from Mr. Gladstone was brought to him for interpretation.

That the German language has become so very popular in College is due to its genial professor, Dr. Sells. He is a splendid lecturer, and does not despise a story or a joke by way of illustration. He has a very un-German abhorrence of tobacco.

DR. DOWDEN, PROFESSOR OF ENGLISH LITERATURE.

Mr. Starkie, one of the most recently elected Fellows, was

educated at Clongowes Wood College, Shrewsbury School, and Trinity College, Cambridge. He is something of a dilettante and is a good judge of pictures. He is, moreover, a great traveller, knows Rome, perhaps, better than he knows Dublin; has mused amidst the ruins of the Acropolis; has swum in the Dead Sea; and taken photographs by the lake of Gennesaret.

The following doggerel verses have a local interest:—

> There is an ancient College, lads,
>   Well known to you and me,
> They call that ancient College, lads,
>   By the name of T.C.D.
>
> Now if you have the time, my boys,
>   I'll unto you rehearse
> The worthies of that ancient place,
>   Done into doggerel verse.
>
> We're ruled by seven worthy men,
>   Who *wise* men once have been;
> In lucid moments they toss up,
>   And choose a Junior Dean.
>
> Now some they paint the Dean most black,
>   Some paint him white alway;
> Just now he's neither white nor black,
>   But plain Tom Thompson Gray.
>
> George Salmon can both preach and sing,
>   And calculate his tail,
> A fish of great capacity,
>   As great as Jonah's whale.
>
> Some say that Poole's a puddle, boys,
>   But please God they're astray,
> He surely had his pupils once
>   A credit in their way.
>
> Sam Haughton is a wily man,
>   Of scientific scope,
> And yet we know he'd hang himself
>   If he had but the rope.
>
> Mahaffy every tongue can speak;
>   He's cosmopolitan,
> And that, you know, is only Greek
>   To a pure-bred Irishman.
>
> Enough of wild, original minds
>   That only raise hubbubs;
> Oh, give to me the genial soul
>   Of calm, star-gazing Stubbs.

"Who fears to speak of ninety-eight?"
   And who will Ingram blame? - -
Whose glorious song dispelled the night
   That shrouded Ireland's fame.

Joe Carson smiles a pleasant smile
   When his intents are ill ;
He plays the devil with men's hopes,
   And smiles most gaily still.

There is a keen-eyed, witty wight,
   Who knows what is the law,
And when he passes some say d—n,
   And others " Doctor Shaw."

Bob Tyrrell is our Cicero
   His Latin is not worse ;
And when he rhymes in English 'tis
   But Ciceronian verse.

Our Palmer is a scholar, too,
   Who oft in days of old
Stood up, like the Apostle, with
   The eleven, and was bowled.

Fitzgerald knows the laws of light,
   And lightly vaults the rail ;
His lady love's a mermaid fair,
   And thereby hangs a tale

A sportsman, too, is Anthony,
   A shot that cannot fail :
Great Jove alone can save the birds
   When he is on the *trail*.

Oh ! Burnside is a jolly man,
   And Burnside loves a horse;
He takes things always as they come,
   And nothing bars his course.

Some would they were Inquisitors,
   With Abbott on the rack ;
Some would that they were pitchforks,
   And pitching into Stack.

George Cathcart out of Hall's not bad,
   Yet a Judas beard has he ;
Some say the devil gives him tips
   In Trigonometry.

Whenever Conner walks abroad,
   In sunshine or in fog,
In Sackville street or College square,
   There follows Conner's dog.

Now some they say he owns the dog,
   And some the dog owns him ;
But one thing's sure, they'll never part
   Till torn limb from limb.

Last night I heard two cats discourse
  Upon the shortest way,
To find their locus on the leads,
  And one said, "Ask M'Cay.

CHORUS.

Sing Rah ; sing Rah for good old T.C.D.;
  Sing Rah ; sing Rah for Dublin Varsity,
Drown Classics, Mathematics,
  And drown Philosophy,
In a jorum of punch till the morning.

CHAPTER VII.

ἄνθρωπος φύσει πολιτικὸν ζῶον.

THE COLLEGE HISTORICAL SOCIETY.

BEFORE the present Historical Society was founded several other societies of the kind had existed in Trinity College. The philosopher Berkeley had formed a small private society for the discussion of philosophical subjects; and in 1747 Edmund Burke, then a Scholar, and in his Senior Sophister year, instituted a Society for the cultivation of composition, history, and oratory. Of this Society Goldsmith was a member. It is not known how long it lasted, but Burke took his degree in 1751, and it is probable that the Society declined after he left College. In 1753 Barry Yelverton, afterwards Lord Avonmore, founded a Historical Club, but of its proceedings no record remains. Yelverton was well qualified to be the president of a debating society; his oratory was magnificent. Grattan, when speaking of the Penal Code, refers thus to a speech of Yelverton's delivered in 1782 in support of the Roman Catholic claims:—" It," the Penal Code, "was detailed by the late Lord Avonmore—I heard him—his speech was the whole of the subject, and a concatenated and inspired argument, not to be resisted; it was the march of an elephant, it was a wave of the Atlantic, a column of water 3,000 miles deep. He began with the Catholic at his birth, he followed him to his grave; he showed that, in every period, he was harassed by the law—the law stood at his cradle, it stood at his bridal bed, it stood at his coffin."

In June, 1757, an attempt seems to have been made unsuccessfully to unite Yelverton's Club with the older one founded by Burke. How long either of these clubs lasted we have no means of judging, but it is probable that the present Historical Society, founded in 1770, owes its origin to Yelverton's Club. The year 1770 was no inopportune time for the forming of a debating society. All Ireland, and Dublin especially, were full of political excitement. The efforts of Lucas and his associates were giving evidences of that spirit which, in 1782, was to hail with joy and delight the bright dawn of freedom, and the popular mind was filled with dreams of glory and independence.

The first volume of the proceedings of the Historical Society is unfortunately lost, so that we are left without information as to who were the founders, and whether it was immediately connected with the societies formerly existing. Grattan is said to have been a member, but that is doubtful. We know that he was in Dublin in the spring of 1770, though no longer in College. At the end of March he went to England to study law. His son, Henry, won a medal for Composition in the Society, and we have a letter extant from his father congratulating him on his success. In his *Historical Sketches of the Statesmen who flourished in the time of George III.*, Lord Brougham states that both Grattan and Flood were members of the Historical. Curran was a scholar in 1770, and may have belonged to the Society. In 1773 the Society was firmly established, and the average attendance of members amounted to upwards of eighty.

The following extract from Mr. Ball's opening address in 1774 may give some notion of the debates at the time:—" One gentleman arises and opens the debate by modestly informing the Society that 'he has nothing to say, for that indeed he has not studied the question,' and sits down. Another arises to oppose the last, and to that purpose, with equal modesty, assures us that 'the arguments of his learned and respectable friend, who opened the debate, carry with them such weight and authority, 'twould be presumption in him to attempt an answer, and—besides—indeed, being prevented by necessary avocations, *he* has not studied the question either', and he sits down. The President, after some minutes spent in the most awkward silence imaginable, is forced to rise and put the question to the vote. . . . Well may Oxford, well may Cambridge, make their boast, and call us, as they do, 'their Silent Sister!' Shamefully indolent as we are, the reproaches of these might rouse us. Seats of a confined and monkish learning, shall they produce wits, and poets, and orators, while the only seminary for the education of gentlemen in Europe is barren of these fruits? Forbid it glory; Forbid it patriotism! Forbid it shame! That the soil which reared a Burke, the soil which produced an Hussey, should cease on a sudden, that fertility from which fame has fondly promised herself to gather for futurity the richest present she ever made it." But this order of things was happily soon to pass away. It was but the darkest hour before the dawn of such glorious names as Grattan, Curran, Plunket, Bushe, and Moore. The journals of the Society break off here until we come to the—to Irishmen—ever-memorable year 1782. At no time could the society boast of possessing so many distinguished members. If in the "Old House" across the way the eloquence of a Grattan and a Flood won the admiration of an astonished world, inside the walls of old Trinity a Plunket, a Bushe, a Magee, the Emmets, and Tone contended for the palm of victory. These were indeed the halcyon days of the society, as they were of Ireland. Then the gown was the only passport required by Trinity men to gain admission to the Gallery of the House of Commons, and it is not to be wondered that their lips caught some of the divine fire from the splendid orations of Grattan, Flood, or Curran. *Primi inter pares* of the members of the Historical at this time were Plunket, who was proposed for membership in 1782 by Thomas Addis Emmett, and won several medals for oratory and composition; Charles Kendal Bushe, afterwards Chief Justice of Ireland, of whom Grattan, having heard him speak at the Society's debates, declared that "he spoke with the lips of an angel;" Peter Burrowes, who with Curran defended the state prisoners in the trials which followed the Rebellion of 1798. Many a story is told of his mental abstraction. On one occasion he was found by his comrades standing with an egg in his hand, and his watch boiling on the fire. Next comes Temple Emmet, who died young. Of him Mr. George Miller, in his speech from the chair of the Society, spoke thus:—" Even now the well-earned applause of this assembly is not confined within these walls. We have seen it give an early celebrity to the abilities of a man, who, in his short but honourable career, adorned the profession of an advocate with the brilliancy of genius and the varied erudition of a scholar." The oratory of his more famous brother—Robert Emmet—was as brilliant as his life was unfortunate, but it was more earnest and had less of the Asiatic style which characterised Temple Emmet's speeches. Thomas Addis Emmet was also an able debater though less vehement than either of his brothers. But, perhaps, the most distinguished of the members of the Historical, about this time, was Theobald Wolfe Tone. He was elected Auditor in 1785. Referring to his

THEOBALD WOLFE TONE.
Auditor 1785.

College career, he writes in his *Autobiography* :—" As it was, however, I obtained a Scholarship, three premiums, and three medals from the Historical Society—a most admirable institution—of which I had the honour to be Auditor, and also to close the session with a speech from the chair, the highest compliment which that Society was used to bestow." On quitting office he was voted the marked thanks of the Society for " his very faithful and attentive discharge of the duties of that office " A remarkable proof of his popularity and the esteem in which he was held was given when, on being robbed of the three medals he had obtained from the Society, it was moved by Plunket and seconded by Magee, that he should be presented "with three medals in the place of those which he had been robbed of, as well to testify our respect for so valuable a member, as because we would wish to perpetuate the proofs of our own discernment." But I have been tempted to linger, perhaps too long, among these remarkable men who belonged to the Society at this, its brightest and most flourishing period. It may be interesting, however, to give some of the topics discussed in the Society at this time, as indications of the disposition of mind of its members. Among them we find such questions as— "Whether an act Declaratory of the Rights of Ireland would be at Present for its Advantage?" and "Could Ireland Exist as a Free State, Independent of any other Nation," in which question Thomas Addis Emmet took the negative side; " Whether Ireland, if Refused the Lately Demanded Constitutional Equality, would be Justifiable in Breaking off her Connexion with Great Britain?" This question was carried unanimously in the affirmative, no one attempting to take the negative side. The feeling of the members of the Society may likewise be gathered from an order to the Librarian "to procure ten copies of Mr. Grattan's Speech on the 16th of April, 1782, in which the Rights of Ireland are so ably asserted." And, again, a resolution was passed, "That a poem signed Brutus, containing very unjust and scandalous abuse of the Volunteers of Ireland, and also the most unjust calumny of several private characters, be burned by the hands of the porter in the presence of the Society."

Laurence Parsons, afterwards Earl of Rosse, was elected Auditor for the year 1783, he being at the same time Member of Parliament for the University; nor was he the only Member of Parliament who remained also a member of the Society, for we find, later, John Maxwell obtaining leave of absence during the sitting of Parliament.

In this year (1783) a committee was formed to consider the advisability of admitting Members of the Speculative Society of Edinburgh into the Historical Society.

The Speculative Society was founded in 1764, and numbered amongst its members some of the most brilliant men that Scotland has produced, such as Dugald Stewart, Walter Scott, Jeffrey, Francis Horner, Sir James Mackintosh, and Benjamin Constant. Scott was for some years Secretary, and Jeffrey describes him thus:—" His constant good temper softened the asperities of debate; while his multifarious lore, and the quaint humour which enlivened its display, made him more a favourite as a speaker than some whose powers of debate were far above his. I remember being struck, the first night I spent at the Speculative, with the singular appearance of the Secretary, who sat gravely at the bottom of the table, in a huge woollen nightcap, and, when the President took the chair, pleaded a bad toothache as his apology for coming into that worshipful assembly in such a portentous machine." Jeffrey was so struck by the Essay on Ballads which Scott read that night that he asked to be introduced to him. He found him next evening "in a small den on the sunk floor of his father's house in George-square, surrounded with dingy books." This was the beginning of that warm friendship which united the two most distinguished literary men in Scotland at the time.

Sir James Mackintosh writes of his contemporaries at the Speculative :—" Upon the whole, they were a combination of young men more distinguished than are usually found in one University at the same time, and the subsequent fortune of some of them, almost as singular as their talents, is a curious specimen of the revolutionary times in which I have lived. When I was in Scotland in 1801, Constant was a Tribune in France; Charles Hope, Lord Advocate; and Emmet, his former companion, a prisoner under his control."

But let us return to the Historical Society. It was decided by the committee appointed for the consideration of the question that the members of the Speculative be regarded as privileged members of the Society. In 1785, Bushe, who had joined the Society the previous year, was chosen to close the Summer Session with an address from the chair. He spoke strongly in favour of prepared speeches, against which a prejudice had always existed in the Society. A few of his remarks on the subject are worth quoting :—" For what can be more absurd than to suppose that in a public speech, the nature of which is to exhibit the subject in every light it can admit of, a man can treat a question admitting of a variety of considerations (though perfectly unprepared for its discussion) in as able a manner as if the composition had been the result of mature thought and accurate preparation. . . . . I shall now conclude with expressing my most anxious hopes, my most ardent wishes, that this Society, instituted by the youth of the Irish Nation for the advancement of useful and ornamental knowledge, and the encouragement of every noble passion of the human mind, may long—nay ever—continue to be the honour of its founders, the pride of its members, and a public benefit to their country."

Here we regretfully take our leave of the Society in its brightest days of prosperity and renown, for owing to the loss of another volume of the Journals we have nothing to guide us till we come to the year 1793. Plunket, Bushe, and their contemporaries are gone, their place being taken by such men as Kyle (afterwards Provost), Bishop Jebb, Chief Justice Lefroy, Lord Caulfield, the Hon. Mr. Burke, and John Latouche, afterwards M.P. for Dublin.

In Provost Hutchinson, whatever may have been his faults, the Society had a staunch friend and supporter, and but for his illness and subsequent death, the crisis which threatened the existence of the Society might have been, at least for a time, averted. The members of the Board were never at any time inclined to encourage free and independent thought amongst the students; and not having been in their youth members of the Society, they had no sympathy with or affection for it. One is not therefore surprised that the relations between the Board and the Society, which had never been very cordial, should have resulted in an open rupture, owing to which the Historical left the College and established itself in the city as an external Society. The imprudence of some members of the Society gave the Board an opportunity which they were not slow to avail themselves of. One evening, during the long vacation, Mr. Miller, the then Junior Dean, perceived with horror and amazement a hackney coach drive into the Square, and three young men, whom he had no difficulty in recognising, alight from it, accompanied by two females. He at once laid the matter before the Board, who issued an order that the offenders were no longer to be admitted within the precincts of the College. When the meetings of the Historical Society were resumed in the following Term, the Dean, who happened to attend as an *ex-officio* member, recognised one of the delinquents present, and requested the Auditor to have him removed. But both the Auditor and the Chairman declined to interfere, and the Dean then applying to the offender personally, the latter rose and left rather than involve the Society in a dispute with the University authorities. The Society, fancying its rights invaded, appointed a committee to inquire into the affair. Incensed at this, which he considered an aspersion on his character as Dean, Mr. Miller laid the matter before the Board, who drew up a code of more stringent rules, which amongst other things, forbade anyone to remain a member of the Society whose name was no longer on the College books. It was also commanded that the name of the proposer of the inquiry into the Dean's conduct should be erased from the list of the Society. To these commands a committee of the Society returned a dignified and temperately worded protest, pointing out that the Board were mistaken as to its object, which was to discover the reason of a member being obliged to retire from their meetings. A hope was also expressed that the Board would not insist that the name of the proposer be erased from the books. The Committee showed, too, that the order for the exclusion of the extern members would be destructive to the prosperity of the Society, and prayed the Board to reconsider its decision. On receipt of this reply, the Board resumed possession of the Society's rooms, declaring that it was more than ever convinced of the impropriety of allowing extern members to attend the meetings of the Society.

To any of the students who might wish to meet, subject to such restrictions as the Board should think proper to prescribe, they offered the use of the rooms. On this, the Society adjourned to the Assembly Rooms in William Street, and drew up an appeal to the Provost, in which they informed him of the particulars of the dispute. The concessions which they had offered proceeded, they said, as far as was consistent with the spirit of gentlemen and the honour of a Society which aspired to his protection. No reply seems to have been received to this address, which may be accounted for by the illness of the Provost, who died in the following September.

The hostility of the Board did not end here. Students were forbidden by a decree to attend any meeting held outside the walls for the purpose of debate. Considerable attention was excited by this dispute; and the Society received many assurances of sympathy and support, not merely from members present, but also from those who retained an affectionate and grateful recollection of the advantages which they had derived from the Society. Mr. Evans, one of the former members, offered to place a sum of money at their disposal, if it were needed; but this generous offer was thankfully declined. A number of past members, resident in London, held a meeting at the Crown and Rolls, Chancery Lane, and there drew up an address, thanking the Society for the courageous and manly stand they had made, and promising any assistance in their power. From the Speculative Society of Edinburgh, too, on laying the matter before them, they received a very friendly communication, signed F. Jeffrey, President, and Walter Scott, Secretary, in which they stated that they did not conceive the original compact of 1783 in any way affected by the circumstances announced by the Historical Society. But the dispute was not confined to decrees of the Board or resolutions of the Society. The Press took up sides in the matter, and many were the squibs which appeared. One of these, quoted by Madden in his "Life of Emmet," is remarkable for its bitter irony:—

"At a full meeting of the Vintners, Publicans and Hetaerae in the City of Dublin, held the 1st of May, 1794—Mrs. Margaret Leeson in the chair—Resolved :

"1st. That the thanks of this meeting be presented to the Vice-Provost and Senior Fellows of Trinity College, Dublin, for their public spirited suppression of the Historical Society.

"2nd. That the said Society has considerably injured our respective trades, by employing the Gentlemen of the University (formerly their best customers) one whole evening in the week in Literary pursuits, and wasting many other evenings in preparation for it.

"3rd. That the kind interference of the College must cause the Custom of the College to return gradually to us, and the time of the young gentlemen to be more profitably employed than in the pursuits of the said Institution.

"That the Provost and Senior Fellows be made free of our Society, and that the freedom of the same be presented to them in a quicksilver box.

"Mrs. Leeson having left the chair, and Mrs. Simpson being called thereto, resolved—

"That the thanks of this meeting be given to Mrs. Leeson for her very proper conduct in the chair.

"(Signed by order),

"CATHERINE GRANT, Secretary."

After leaving College, the Society continued to meet for a

considerable time, but gradually the members dropped off, and as the intern Society increased both in numbers and distinction, the old Society gradually declined. In 1806 a meeting was called, and it was resolved to hand over the journals, and other property, to the intern Society. Thus, by the wanton persecution of the Board, ended the career of a society which has shed an undying glory on a University which, up to that time, had done comparatively little to merit honour or distinction.

Soon after the new Society was founded, its members presented a petition to the Board, praying that some of the stringent rules which they had accepted as the charter of their existence might be relaxed. The Board yielded, so far as allowing a few of the former members, whose names were no longer on the College books, to continue as honorary members of the Society. Amongst those who took advantage of this privilege were Plunket, Peter Burrowes, and Richard Jebb. One of the most prominent members of the Society, which soon began to rival its exiled predecessor, was Hugh George Macklin, afterwards Advocate-General at Bombay. From his habit of boasting, he acquired the nickname of "Hugo Grotius Braggadocio." He had considerable facility as a writer of verses, and not unfrequently turned that talent to account. It was said of him, that whenever he found himself hard pressed for money—which happened not seldom—his last resource was to threaten to publish his poems, and this threat brought all his friends to his relief. His boasting powers were unrivalled, and once on the eve of a great public examination, when he was asked if he was well prepared in his conic sections. "Prepared!" he exclaimed, "I could whistle them." Some time after, in a mock account of a night's proceedings in the Historical Society, one of the fines enforced for disorderly conduct was recorded as follows:—"Hugo Grotius Braggadocio, fined one shilling for whistling conic sections." In November, 1797, Thomas Moore became a member of the Society, and a few days after, a name—ever memorable in the annals of Ireland—that of Robert Emmet—was added. A warm friendship sprang up between the two, which lasted until the melancholy and untimely death of the latter. I take the following extract from Moore's *Journal*, as giving some notion of the party feeling which existed within the Society:—" The political ferment that was abroad through Ireland soon found its way within the walls of the University,

and a youth destined to act a melancholy, but ever memorable,
part in the troubled scenes that were fast approaching, now began
to attract in no ordinary degree the attention both of his fellow-
students, and the College authorities in general. This youth was
Robert Emmet, whose brilliant success in his College studies,
and more particularly in the scientific portion of them, had
crowned his career, as far as he had gone, with all the honours of
the course; while his powers of oratory displayed at a debating
society of which, about this time, 1796-7, I became a member,
were beginning to excite universal attention, as well from the
eloquence as the political boldness of his displays. . . . .
Of the popular side in the (Historical) Society the chief champion
and ornament was Robert Emmet; and though every care was
taken to exclude from among the subjects of debate all questions
likely to trench upon the politics of the day, it was always easy
enough, by a side-wind of digression or allusion, to bring Ireland
and the prospects then opening upon her within the scope of
the orator's view. So exciting and powerful in this respect were
the speeches of Emmet, and so little were the most distinguished
speakers among our opponents able to cope with his eloquence,
that the Board at length actually thought it right to send among
us a man of advanced standing in the University, and belonging
to a former race of good speakers in the Society, in order that
he might answer the speeches of Emmet, and endeavour to
obviate what they considered the mischievous impressions produced by them. In his "Life of Lord Edward Fitzgerald,"
Moore thus describes the appearance and manner of Emmet in
the Society:—

"Simple in all his habits, and with a repose of look and
manner indicating but little movement within, it was only when
the spring was touched that set his feelings, and, through them,
his intellect in motion, that he at all rose above the level of
ordinary men. On no occasion was this more peculiarly striking
than in these displays of oratory with which both in the Debating
and Historical Society he so often enchained the attention and
sympathy of his young audience. No two individuals, indeed,
could be much more unlike each other than was the same youth
to himself *before* rising to speak and *after*—the brow that had
appeared inanimate and drooping at once elevating itself in all
the consciousness of power, and the whole countenance and
figure of the speaker assuming a change, as of one suddenly

inspired. Of his oratory, it must be recollected, I speak from youthful impressions, but I have heard little since that appeared to me of a loftier or (what is a far more rare quality in Irish eloquence) purer character; and the effects it produced, as well from its own exciting power as from the susceptibility with which his audience caught up every allusion to passing events, was such as to attract at last seriously the attention of the Fellows."

The poet Moore himself was no mean orator. He is thus described by a contemporary in College:—" Our young hero's next display was in Trinity College, Dublin, where he entered a pensioner. The Historical Debating Society was then in full health and vigour. Young Moore, in his first speech, made an impression on the Auditors that engaged their attention, and struck deeper at every successive debate. He invited me to his rooms in College to hear him and his fellow-students at rehearsal. Their compositions were exceedingly clever; but my friend had the best, and his delivery was easy and natural, much superior to any that competed with him; his speeches had all the effect of extemporary effusions." But the friendly discussions of the Society were destined soon to be interrupted. Rumours of a French invasion to be expected at any moment were rife, and towards the end of 1796 a private meeting was held in College, at which resolutions were passed expressing a desire on the part of some students to arm in defence of their country. They promised that their academic duties should not be interfered with with by their military avocations. When these resolutions were laid before the Chancellor of the University he refused his consent, holding that by such a proceeding the literary pursuits of the students would be interrupted. On the 26th of December a second application was made for permission to arm; and on the 9th of January, 1797, the College Corps received their arms from the Government. They chose four captains and eight lieutenants, all of the former and two of the latter being Fellows of the College, and they selected for their uniform scarlet faced with blue, without any lace, and plain gilt buttons, white Kerseymere waistcoat and breeches, with black leggings.

On the 30th May the Historical Society adjourned till the autumn. On reassembling, amongst those proposed for membership were John Wilson Croker, the Rev. Charles Maturin, and the Rev. George Crolly. In 1804 Charles Phillips became a member, and two years later Henry Grattan was proposed. An attempt was made to have the latter admitted without the usual ballot, as a tribute of respect to his father, but the proposal was negatived by a small majority.

In November, 1809, Richard Lalor Shiel joined the Society, and writing in after life he bears the following important testimony to the advantages of such a Society:—" But with all its imperfections it must be recollected that such an institution affords an occasion for the practice of public speaking, which is as much, perhaps, the result of practical acquisition as it is of natural endowment. A false ambition of ornament might prevail in its assemblies, and admiration might be won by verbose extravagance and boisterous inanity, but a man of genius must still have turned such an institution to account.

"He must have thrown out a vast quantity of ore, which time and circumstances would afterwards separate and refine. His faculties must have been put into action, and he must have learned the art, as well as tasted the delight, of stirring the

ISAAC BUTT.
Auditor 1833.

hearts and exalting the minds of a large concourse of men. The physique of oratory too, if I may use the expression, must have been acquired; a just sense of the value of gesture and intonation result from the practice of public speaking, and the appreciation of their importance is necessary for their attainment."

About this time Charles Wolfe, the author of the famous poem on the burial of Sir John Moore, joined the Society, and in 1814 was chosen to close the Winter Session with a speech from the chair, for which he received a gold medal from the Society. In 1815 the Historical was for the second time in-

THOMAS DAVIS.
Auditor 1838.

volved in a contention with the authorities. A personal dispute unfortunately occurred between two members, and taking advantage of this the Board issued a series of resolutions, which among other things commanded that a committe of five should be appointed to take entire management of the private business of the Society. The hours for their meetings were, also, to be limited, and, what was of most importance to the Society, Junior Sophisters were excluded from membership. The Society appealed against these regulations, through the Committee which had just been formed by order of the Board, and as the latter was unshaken in its determination, it was moved by one of the members "That a Committee of seven be appointed for the purpose of resigning into the custody of the Provost and Board the rooms hitherto appropriated to the use of the Historical Society, the late regulations of the Board being, in the opinion of the Society, inconsistent with the successful prosecu-

W. MacNEILE DIXON.
Auditor 1891.

tion of the objects for which it was instituted; and that this Committee be empowered and directed to take such steps as to them may appear most effectual for the securing the property of the Society until a favourable opportunity occurs for the revival of the Institution, the utility of which the experience of twenty years has most satisfactorily evinced." The motion was passed on a division, after a long and stormy debate, by

50 to 14, and on February 1st, 1815, the Society adjourned *sine die*.

The Historical still continued to meet outside the walls of the College. In 1833 Isaac Butt occupied the chair of the Society, and in the following year was chosen Auditor. Thomas MacNevin was Auditor in 1837, and was succeeded by Thomas Davis. David Pigot was the last Auditor of the Extern Society. On the revival of the Intern Society in 1843, Mr. Foote handed over to the Secretary the property of the Society which remained in his possession. The first Auditor of the Intern Society was Richard Connor Magee, late Archbishop of York, the only Dublin University man ever preferred to an English Archiepiscopal see. Edward Gibson, Baron Ashbourne, the President of the Society, was Auditor in 1858-59.

Mr. MacNeile Dixon, Auditor 1891-92, as an elegant scholar, an admirable speaker, and above all things a courteous gentleman, is no unworthy successor to an office held by some of the most brilliant men whom Ireland has produced.

It was no part of my original intention to do more than give a slight sketch of this Society of great traditions, but I have been impelled by the charm of the subject to deal with it at greater length than the consciousness of my inability to do it justice would otherwise have allowed.

THE PHILOSOPHICAL SOCIETY.

If most of the glory of the Historical belong to the past, that of the Philosophical is entirely of the present. It was founded in 1853, and was called the Undergraduate Philosophical Society. In point of numbers and prosperity it has become a formidable rival of the Historical, most of whose distinguished members graduated in the Philosophical. At the opening meeting of the Society, held in December, 1891, Professor Dowden, a former President, in moving " That the University Philosophical Society is worthy of the support of the students of this University," said the career of the Society was a much shorter one than that of the sister Society, the Historical, but although it was still in its thirties, and its jubilee year was not very near, it could point to many distinguished sons. If he was not mistaken, Mr. Quinton, whose name had been so mournfully enrolled of late on the bead-roll of distinguished Anglo-Indians, was an officer of the Society in its early days.

About the time that he (Professor Dowden) was an undergraduate, one of their Presidents was a most eloquent and ardent youth—Godfrey Pope—a distinguished scholar, who had since surveyed mankind from China to Peru, and from Rameses the First to Mr. Gladstone, perhaps the last. Mr. Mahaffy was also a President. Sir Robert Ball, his successor, had since annexed the starry heavens, and had surveyed the sky from Mercury to Sirius, and made the Milky Way an appendix of Trinity College, Dublin—a mere extension of the College Park. He (Professor Dowden) was a secretary of the Philosophical Society, and he was proud also of the fact that he once occupied the same position that Mr. Smyth occupied that evening. One stalwart member, as he recalled, from the wilds of Connemara or Kerry, was accustomed to come to their meetings armed to the teeth—not with a small horsewhip, but with the poker of his College rooms. He breathed forth threatening and slaughter against them. He, with his poker, was not a popular member. With infinite trouble, if he remembered aright, they succeeded in expelling him. Yet so pleasant were his recollections of those early days that some time since he renewed his intercourse with him (Professor Dowden) by letter, with the amiable object of calling his attention to the disgraceful position he occupied in appearing at a banquet held in honour of Mr. Balfour.

J. W. Quinton was President of the Society in 1855-56. In 1858-59 Professor J. P. Mahaffy occupied the chair. Sir Robert Ball was elected President for the year 1860-61, the office being held in 1863-64 by Professor Dowden. Professor Armstrong, of Cork, author of the "Tercentenary Ode," was chosen to fill the chair in 1867-68. Besides the above-mentioned, the following gained distinction in the Society for Oratory or Composition:—Isaac Ashe, W. H. S. Monck, John Todhunter, W. A. Macdonald, Standish O'Grady, William Wilde, John Ross, G. N. Plunkett, W. F. Starkie, G. D. Burtchaell, J. W. Rolleston, W. F. Bailey, C. H. Oldham, W. M. Dixon, G. F. Brunskill, R. C. K. Wilson, Ernest F. Leet, Cecil Harmsworth, Chas. Smith, W. Innes Pocock, &c. The Society also offers annually for competition a Silver Medal for Aesthetics. It was won in 1890-91 by J. R. O'Connell.

It used to be the custom to keep an Occasional Book in the

Society's Rooms, to which the members contributed, chiefly in verse. Most of these compositions were purely local, and have

T. J. SMYTH.
President 1891.

now lost most of their interest; but I extract one as a specimen of the muse fostered in the Philosopical Society:

VIRGIL.

Virgil, whose magic verse enthrals—
    And who in verse is greater?
By turns his wandering hero calls
    Now "Pius," and now "Pater."

But when prepared the worst to brave,
    An action that must pain us,
Queen Dido meets him in the cave,
    He dubs him "Dux Trojanus."

And well he changes thus the word:
    On that occasion, sure,
"Pius Aeneas" were absurd,
    And *Pater* premature.

The Philosophical Society is a miniature Parliament, and often there is a strong Opposition party to the Government. During the Session 1885-86, I remember, the Opposition was very strong—so strong, indeed, that it was almost impossible to get any business done. Paddy Branagan was leader of the intellectual portion of the Opposition, and he was supported by a stalwart called M'Hardy, who led the Opposition physical force party. For a time the officers and Council were wholly unable to cope with their opponents. Paddy Branagan held the floor every night, supported by M'Hardy's band; and the hall where the meetings were held became a veritable pandemonium. Finally, the Council decided to adopt extreme measures. They packed the meeting one night with the sturdiest members of the Boat Club and Football Club. At a given signal these fell, with one consent, on M'Hardy and his band, and after a brief but desperate struggle, ejected them. Paddy, although compelled to adopt a more constitutional course, still remained a thorn in the side of the Council; but the proceedings of the Society were much more orderly than before.

R. H. WOODS.

A few years ago, a very clever skit was read before the Society by R. H. Woods, entitled, "The Spirit of the Times."

It was "written with the object of satirising a style adopted by some debating Society essayists, by which they obtain, at the expense always of clearness and generally of good sense, a reputation for profundity through using terms and forms of speech with which the essayists themselves, are unfamiliar." During the reading of the paper the Hall was crowded by an attentive audience, few of whom suspected that they were being

C. W. WILSON.
Ex-President, and joint author with R. H. Woods, of the College Tercentenary farce, "Botany Bay."

made the victims of a practical joke. Many eloquent speeches were delivered at the conclusion of the paper, some by members of the Society who were in the secret and had co-operated in perpetrating the essay, and others who believed it to be a serious effort. One gentleman while accepting as true all the other statements made in the essay, refused to admit that " what is to be, will be, as surely and as certainly, as what has been, surely and certainly was to be."

A few extracts from the essay itself will give a better notion of the style than any description could possibly do. "The malignant cacology of disappointed ambition, and the pusillanimous snarlings of hypocritical sycophancy, only serve to bring into more effectual contrast the rhythmic motion of the billows of the ocean of veracity. The purgatorial apopthegms of a theophagous Monotheism, indefeasible, as they may be, fail to pardon, or even to palliate the wild outcries of an ejaculatory enthusiam.

"The self-appointed apostles of modern reform, such artificial luminaries in the Radical firmament as Charles Bradlaugh and Mrs. Besant in England, and Col. Robert Ingersoll in America, have not even had the wit to see that the arrogant interposition of factitious distinctions between the classes and masses, while it has the manifest advantage of interpenetrating, and to a certain extent relieving the insipid monotony which would inevitably arise under conditions that did not permit the mutual action and reaction involved in those very presuppositions, without which even the contemplation of such conditions becomes itself a mere play of the imagination, is nevertheless attended with the counterbalancing disadvantage that it leaves out of sight one of the most weighty factors of the cosmical equation, viz., the innate inebriety of mankind."

"The vulgar herd place their happiness in the applause of crowds, in earthly honours, in the bubble reputation, and think it cheap if obtained 'even at the cannon's mouth;' and if their fellows are indiscriminate and ungenerous, with blasted hopes and disappointed expectancies, they pass to an ignoble grave, 'unwept, unhonoured, and unsung.' It is far otherwise with those who seek a glimpse, however transitory, of the sublime features of the goddess of Truth ; their reward, which no man hath given unto them, no man shall take from them."

> "By what extreme or unimpassioned border,
> Disrobed of thunder, by the storms unriven,
> We marshalled in environing disorder,
> Who see but with Life's dark mysterious glasses
> The weird stars in the trenchant night of Heaven,
> 'Neath th' unimagined eyes of that grim warder,
> While all the loud vacuities are numb,
> Th' abysmal gulphs, where evermore we've striven,
> Whilom bereft their nameless army passes
> Forlorn, innumerous dumb."

These remarkable verses were composed by Mr. W. Innes Pocock, who in the course of his speech, with admirable modesty, expressed his regret that the essayist had omitted the context and thereupon proceeded to quote the following lines:—

> "So roll the hungering years, a hundred millions
> Smirching the pureness of their margent snows,
> Dead years, resistless to their white pavilions,

> O'ercanopied as that tremendous legion,
> And charactered like music's mourning close,
> Fold over fold, a river-shining region,
> In still contention of outworn repose."

These verses were described by a modern critic as " a passage of singular beauty, though of great obscurity, by reason of its far-fetched metaphors and extraordinary involution of style."

My publisher insists on my concluding here, but before doing so I wish to say a few words on the decadence of oratory in Dublin University. I believe this is due chiefly to the exclusion of politics from the Societies' debates. It is impossible that the blood of youth should be stirred by the dry bones of dead theories, nor does a debate on the Labour Movement wake enthusiasm any more than a discussion on the rival merits of poets or philosophers. In the old days of the Irish Parliament, the burning questions debated in College Green, were discussed with hardly less eloquence and force by the Students of Trinity College. As long as politics are banned, we can have no earnestness, and therefore little eloquence, in the College debates.

FINIS.

www.ingramcontent.com/pod-product-compliance
Lightning Source LLC
Chambersburg PA
CBHW020252090426
42735CB00010B/1889